30 Days of Truth: Waking the Unconscious Soul

30 Days of Truth: Waking the Unconscious Soul

By Kara C. Adams

ISBN 9781070420066

Dedication

The world needs you. This book needs you. Every time a copy of *30 Days of Truth* is sold, lives are being impacted in Mozambique, Africa. **Flourish and Thrive**, located in Mozambique, is a non-profit organization that focuses on teaching orphans different venues of occupation as a means to keep them out of prostitution. The Ladybug Project, founded by Kara and best friend Alyssa Vine-Hodge, raises awareness on child molestation and teams up with organizations like **Flourish and Thrive**. *30 Days of Truth*, as well as other books written by Kara, are ways to support The Ladybug Project. Thank you for being a part of the change this world desperately needs. You've taken action in The Ladybug Project, being a voice for the small and silent with this purchase. To learn more about The Ladybug Project and ways to help those affected by sexual trauma, go to www.karacadams.com

Introduction

Within these covers are 30 truths that have changed my life. I've struggled from child molestation, divorce, parent alienation, death of a loved one, bankruptcy, living out of my car from having no home, and making more than a few bad life choices. For the past 20 years, I've gone to over 10 counselors and read countless "self-help" books to discover these truths that have freed me from what felt like chains. Throughout my life, people have consistently asked: "Where do you get your energy from?" or "How are you so full of joy?" These truths are part of my story of tapping into the peace and joy I have found. My wish for you is that you open your mind and heart to receive the same.

Over the next 30 days, allow each truth to settle deep within the soul and retrain the unconscious (the darkest part of the shadow within). Every truth assist in letting go of pre-existing ideas and eliminating self-sabotage. Success is an option, whichever channel it pertains to-- physically, spiritually, mentally, socially, or financially.

Unwrap these 30 powerful truths, so they become embedded into the unconscious soul....the one that lost its way from the path of the womb to this very present moment. Use them as a tool to break habits and beliefs that have been toxic to the spirit, lies that have been accepted throughout your life.

Read each truth, speak them out loud, use as a daily meditation to focus on, and reflect on throughout the day as a mantra. Study them until the soul's consciousness demands the unconsciousness to be in alignment. If a truth needs to be revisited, do so. Play it over and over again like a broken record, until it registers, even if it takes days or months. Doing so will impact the foundation of your soul, down to the structural molecular level, manifesting the healthiest version of oneself. The true self.

Ready…set…GO!

Day 1

Truth:

I AM LOVABLE

Love is unconditional.
It is freedom beyond the realm that we can and cannot physically see. Love has always been. It always will be, and it is the light that shines through darkness, revealing all truth. I am love. I am loved. I am lovable, and I choose to accept this truth. My heart has known from the beginning, from the formation of my soul, and timeless love made every effort to make sure I came into existence. I am qualified to be me. I belong here. I understand that love inhabits me and that I am here to inhabit this earth. I am the love this space deserves to experience.

Facts:
There is only one me.
I was fearfully and wonderfully made in the womb.
I was created in love, I am surrounded by love, and
I AM LOVE.

Day 2

Truth:

I AM FREE & CHOOSE TO BE ME

I am me, and I am free.
I am capable of doing what I love. I am not subject to another human or under the domination of some other influence. I will explore the freedom I have. I refuse to have strings pulling me in every direction. There is freedom in learning from my triumphs, as well as from my mishaps. As an infant learns to walk yet falls down, he or she never questions: "Why?" He/she doesn't cry, yet simply gets up and tries again. Falling represents progress. Progress leads to growth, and growth turns into prosperity. As a child, I never worried about being or pleasing anyone else. I cried when I felt like crying and laughed when it felt right. I let my emotions be expressed and then moved along. I was flexible, free of expectations, and everything was intriguing because I lived in the moment. Today, I will be me, taking comfort in how I express myself and delighting in my personal rights.

Day 3

Truth:

MY PURPOSE IS DIVINE

My reason for existence is not something to eventually be determined….it is done. I am the result of a direct intention. One of the oldest books in history, the Bible, says in its first book called Genesis, chapter one: "So God created man in His *own* image; in the image of God He created him; male and female He created them. Then God blessed them, and God said to them, 'Be fruitful and multiply; fill the earth and subdue it; have dominion over the fish of the sea, over the birds of the air, and over every living thing that moves on the earth.'"

I am created in God's image. If that isn't divine, then nothing is. Today, I accept that I am like the sun. I show up no matter what. I shine divine, even through the clouds that attempt to block my light. Nothing can hide what God made….the blessing I am and the purpose that I host.

Day 4

I DO MY BEST

I have full ownership of me. I am responsible for my own actions as well as reactions. My personal best cannot compare with anyone else's. My best is like having my own personal background music playing to my daily life routines. My theme song grows louder with each new day. If I feel I'm not my best, I am still doing my best in that situation. Every moment, every day and every season is a path to the best life possible. It won't be tomorrow or years from now. The time is now.

Everyone's best looks different. Every circumstance leads to a different aspect of my best. In each second, I am doing my best. Today, I am bringing my best to the table and my appetite to devour all of its greatness.

Day 5

Truth:

GRATITUDE IS MY ATTITUDE

May every breath remind me to be grateful. Let me seek out the gifts and the blessings, being mindful of the moments I can learn from and aware of the love I can offer. When I direct my thoughts towards an attitude of gratitude, I allow my heart to grow....leaving less room for the darkness that brings about decay. Gratitude opens the doors to victory, a world of opportunities, and spaces of immense light. There is everlasting peace that allows my heart to expand beyond the walls of my flesh. I will allow my soul to sing songs of thanksgiving throughout this day. The more I focus on my blessings, the more they appear. I am grateful to be alive, to breathe, and to celebrate in everything that brings a smile to my face. What an honor to see all the beauty around me. When gratitude is my attitude, I create more space for love and less for sadness or madness.

Today, I wake with a smile on my face and choose to show the world all the love in my heart.

Day 6

Truth:

I PARTICIPATE IN MIRACLES

I am part of an extraordinary event in this physical world that surpasses all known human or natural powers. I am a work of God, which in return makes me a miracle worker. I understand that I am a miracle and my breath matters. I take responsibility for my part, to be the change that I want to see. It is not an accident that I exist. I am part of a phenomenal masterpiece that is being composed. Every note, every string, and every lyric comes together to make a beautiful arrangement. Every note is needed to play the song, my note must be played and not be a missing link. Thus, I participate in the miracle of life and the song of this universe. May I create more miracles today by taking part. I will give. I will help. I will serve. I will choose kindness and love. I participate in miracles because I am one.

Day 7

Truth:

I AM ALWAYS HOME

This body, this shell, is my home.
I can have peace no matter where I am physically, mentally,
spiritually, socially, and financially. Today, I continuously
come back to this thought: I am already home and dwell in a
safe shelter. There is no need to feel lost, disassociated, or
impatient. I am all I need to be complete. I am home where I
was created in love, knit together in detail, and designed
with intention. I welcome the refuge I have to offer my
radiance that this planet desperately needs. Courage exists
within me to rest assured that I am in good hands. This
residence I have real estate in is elite, unavailable for
purchase. I am more than an investment,
I was built on a solid foundation.
I am home.

Day 8

Truth:

IT'S NOT PERSONAL

Whatever other people do is not because of me.
How people behave and act is not mine to judge. Anything
someone says or does is not my reality, but a projection of
theirs. It is their dream they are living out, so it is not mine
to take personally. I must become immune to the opinions of
others, as well as their actions. This will save me from
needless suffering and viewing myself as a victim. This
truth needs to be revisited, perhaps daily. I will be patient in
order to master this truth with myself, because it may take
some time. It is not mine to take personally the behavior
and choices of others.

Day 9

Truth:

I AM WORTHY

Say it and mean it! If I have to think this thought all day, so be it. Because I am worth it! I am worthy of being loved, loving, fulfilling my destiny, and living my best life. Self-worth is vital to understanding my capabilities. My fragrance is enjoyable. My fragrance is the energy I release. I am a satisfying taste and smell. I am as pleasing to this earth as are the flowers and plants that surround me. I am like the four senses: I make a delicate, pleasant sound. My touch is gracious and kind. My body is a fascinating invention, elaborately designed. My thoughts are unlike anyone else's. I will respect myself like an endangered species. I hold worth because I am uncommon, rare and extraordinary. I am of value. I possess great merit. Only I am worthy to facilitate this temple.

Day 10

Truth:

I LET GO

I let go of anything that will keep me from being me. When a plane has too much weight, it cannot take off. The art of letting go of circumstances is mine to embrace, so that it might not interfere with my energy, my presence, and well-being. Today, I will keep my emotions in check and allow the mind to master its power. Surrender does not mean failure. It can lighten my load. Surrendering is a gift. It can induce limitless possibilities. Like animals that shed their exoskeleton, I can let old attachments fall away and walk unencumbered in new directions. Letting go allows more room for a peaceful mind. If I will get out of the way and trust the universe (like nature does), I will feel lighter and learn how to soar. Today, I choose to let go and not carry the burdens of the world or my fears.

"To the ego mind, surrender means giving up.
To the spiritual mind, surrender means
giving in and receiving."
- *The Law of Divine Compensation* by
Marianne Williamson

Day 11

Truth:

THERE IS ALWAYS A WAY

There is always a way, if I am willing to find it.
Solutions exist in abundance. They may not appear the way
I expect them to, and that's why I should clear the narrow
path I've been trained in and allow expansion to occur.
Each individual holds a sliver of perspective.
Openness to shifting my stance, even slightly,
allows more space to see a bigger picture.
I choose to grow today through unlimited
results that may unfold through
unexpected sources. Regardless,
**EVERYTHING ALWAYS WORKS
OUT FOR ME.**

Truth:

I WILL NOT MAKE ASSUMPTIONS

Assuming is a form of arrogance. Recall the saying: "To
assume is to make an 'ass out of you and me'."
Presuming every situation is about me hosts a narcissistic
attitude. I will do my best to choose compassion and
understand that others' circumstances are unique. Each
individual experiences and handles life differently,
so grace must be my prerequisite.
When I assume, I believe something is true without
finding evidence or proof that it is real. Today,
I will seek truth. I will ask or seek further
investigation and not make assumptions.

Day 13

Truth:

I CHOOSE JOY

Joy is satisfying bliss, a state of happiness or felicity. I understand that it is an inside job. Finding happiness (true joy) isn't a secret. The key is within.
The file already exists in my computer. I will pull this file up and use it. I will slow down and practice joy. No human or materialistic thing can take it away from me. My amusement puts others at ease and soothes situations.
Joy is not something to learn ….
it is something to live. I can laugh at life, and
I will seek humor in all I do. Today, I seek joy.
Bringing joy to others is the fastest
path to joy for me.

Day 14

Truth:

THIS TOO SHALL PASS

Every moment is surpassed by another.
There is no need to dwell on circumstances that never seem
to transition. The truth is nothing stays constant. The hard
moments, the beautiful ones, the easy moments, the serious,
funny and challenging moments all eventually become
memories or moments forgotten. Occasionally, the mind
generates illusions that feed a false belief that
I will not escape from a present position.
This is not reality--
The actuality is that this too shall pass. When the wind
blows, if I attempt to catch or control it, then I come across
as one that has 'lost his/her marbles.' If I choose to be
mindful, then I know the wind will eventually stop.
Moments can change because my mind can change. When
my mind changes, it affects everyone around me.
Today, I treasure up for myself moments
that are noble of remembering.

Day 15

Truth:

I AM FORGIVING

To forgive is to pardon an offense or offender.
It is to cancel an indebtedness. God's will is that I forgive
myself. It's not my arrogance, but my humility that teaches
me that who I am is good enough. Forgiveness isn't just
forgiving others. I must also learn to forgive myself and not
be so harsh towards myself when I make a mess. When milk
is spilled, it wasn't my motive to create an accident.
It's part of a process that transpired and results in my
reaction of tidying up. Choosing forgiveness means seeing
an opportunity for growth and not participating in criticism.
Constant judgment can send me into the depths of a
downward spiral, full of self-destruction.
When I give myself permission to forgive myself, forgiving
others becomes second nature. Mishaps happen
for me and for others, too.
Today, I focus on this mantra:
I AM FORGIVING.

Day 16

Truth:

MY WORD IS IMPECCABLE

I will honor what I say, in the words of
Don Miguel Ruiz from his book
The Four Agreements:
"Being impeccable with your word is the correct use of your
energy; it means to use your energy in the direction of truth
and love for yourself. If you make an agreement with
yourself to be impeccable with your word, just with that
intention, the truth will manifest through you and clean all
the emotional poison that exists within you. But making this
agreement is difficult because we
have learned to do precisely the opposite."

My word is a gift. To be impeccable with my word is taking
responsibility for my actions. My word has the power to
create life or death. I can break a curse by making a new
agreement based on truth. The truth can set me free. How
much I love myself and how I feel about myself are directly
proportionate to the quality and integrity of my word. When
I'm impeccable with my word, I feel good;
I feel happy and at peace.

Truth:

I DO NOT JUDGE

I judge people because in some way they
threaten my survival--
Whether it be philosophically, physically, or sexually.
Today, in any moment that I feel I might be casting
judgement, I will say: "I DO NOT JUDGE." I will allow
myself to be mindful and let go of any criticism that has
formed. I will lead with intentions of praise and acceptance.
The way I evaluate others and myself is a discovery of my
influences and behavior. I will seek out how to be neutral
and of a fair-mind.
I will attempt to fix my hardships without force. I choose to
let go of assumptions to keep an open mind. I am open to
understand others as a reflection of their own pain and
judgements. This allows me to not take what they are doing
and saying personally. My study in this is knowing that I am
only responsible for my own reactions. There is a time and
season for everything, including how people treat me. Does
this mean I have to suffer a lifetime for my past decisions?
Even if they were made out of a place of compassion or
misunderstanding? No, it is not in my control whether my
current circumstances are justified or not. Today, I know I
have freedom from others projections and access to
unlimited joy. I breathe in love and breathe out love.
Emotions may come and go, and I will not engage in them.
Yet, I will recognize them. My decision will be to stay
attentive to the present moment and not judge.

Truth:

MONEY IS ENERGY

My subconscious mind sometimes blocks me from unlimited possibilities. Money is like energy and flows; it is a currency that I elect to react negatively, positively, or neutral towards.
Anytime I come face-to-face with putting myself at risk, my subconscious stops me. I must evolve, learn to reprogram the mind. Operate at the highest level of energy available. This will assist in knowing the truth….that money is good, it can be great and fun. This money truth reveals the unnatural I've been taught to believe, that lack and fear is reality.
Functioning at a low frequency, for example; participating in patterns that I'm accustomed to…. produces the same results I've lived through my entire life. If I have trouble saying any of the following affirmations below, then I will say it until it flows easily from my lips and stands true to my core:
"Money flows to and from me easily, I love spending it and I love making it. There is plenty of money to go around. Money is freedom, money is power, and money is my pal. I love money and money loves me. The money I desire is already here. I am energy, money is energy, we are samesies, and we are besties."
-affirmation excerpt from Jen Sincero's
You are a Badass at Making Money

I embrace today's truth: MONEY IS ENERGY.
How I choose to let it flow is up to me.

Truth:

MY BREATH CREATES BALANCE

Balance doesn't just pertain to an equal distribution of weight physically. It is a state of steadiness for the mind. Watching babies learn to crawl and walk reminds me that balance is a constant teacher in life. Falling shows me the principles of why I fall, which helps me gain perspective of how to attain balance.

Balance exists on all pillars of life: physically, spiritually, mentally, financially, and socially. I will ponder on the laws of balance by accepting that my falls are a great way to grow and reach a conscience equilibrium. I acknowledge balance is in the present. The weight of my past verses my unexpected future is not to be the focus.

I live in this moment, which is beyond this hour, surpassing my thoughts, and not concerned with any outcome.

Balance is a harmony. It is the tension I feel within me that forces me to meditate in every movement.

I breathe in balance. I breathe out balance.

The steadiness of my breath creates the relaxation I need to understand the stillness. The stillness that prevails in nature allows me to observe the connection. The connection I have with everyone and everything. It is in the stillness of the soul where enlightenment is found unending.

Day 20

Truth:

I CREATE MY OWN REALITY

Mastering this mindset is a lifelong commitment. I vow to slow down, in order to see how to live a healthy life. I create a life of desire through the way I live. I am creative considering I was created. This shows through in how I: organize the house; make artwork; write; do yard work; or pick out what I'm going to wear. It is in the simple day-to-day activities that I feel accomplished and inspired to create more. I can identify my passions, create myself, and even create healing through my struggles. When struggles do exist, I know that what is built along the way gives meaning to the pain. Switching my perspective from pain to opportunity, or misfortune to gaining wisdom, and perhaps buzzing questions to boundless solutions is the biggest game changer. I will remind myself that the energy used to eat an apple is the same amount of energy that is used to eat a cookie, and that the reality created is made by the decision of what was chosen. I create my own reality by mastering my mindset, changing my daily routine, and understanding that what I do matters. How I spend my energy is the start to my own personal gain, aka success.

Day 21

Truth:

I AM HERE

If I'm here on this planet, born and have breath, I am worthy to be here. I have the opportunity to perform and live out a purpose that no one else has. Planted as a light, I have the beautiful potential of finding my pack of wolves to run with. The earth deserves the whole me. I empower the space I take up. The first cry I let out as an infant when I came out of my mother's womb was my affirmation: "I proclaim I'm here mother earth, hear me roar!" I claimed my space on this earth in that moment, that I matter and my breath is needed.

My formation, the first cell that was used to begin my existence, is my molecular level foundation. Today, I will enjoy the present. And I will be present. This means putting my phone down and being in the moment, and coinciding with conversations that may occur because that moment needs me. Not only are the best memories created this way, but everyone around me is impacted with my presence and will be empowered. As I will be impacted and empowered by their presence.

I matter and will celebrate this!

"Our deepest fear is not that we are inadequate. Our deepest fear is that we are powerful beyond measure. It is our light, not our darkness that most frightens us. We ask ourselves, Who am I to be brilliant, gorgeous, talented, fabulous? Actually, who are you not to be? You are a child of God. You playing small does not serve the world. There is nothing enlightened about shrinking so that other people won't feel insecure around you. We are all meant to shine, as children do. We were born to make manifest the glory of God that is within us. It's not just in some of us; it's in everyone. And as we let our own light shine, we unconsciously give other people permission to do the same. As we are liberated from our own fear, our presence automatically liberates others."

- *A Return to Love* by
Marianne Williamson

Day 22

Truth:

ACCEPTANCE IS MY STRENGTH

Acceptance is the beginning of joy....
a start to happiness. Accepting what is, in every moment,
is meditation. Meditation is the art of now, learning to exist
in every moment. There is no need to react, and I will only
accept. I embrace this strength, as it settles my soul and
allows peace to resonate from the depths of my existence
to the hairs atop my head. Today, I adopt and approve
of my circumstances, respect what may arise,
and honor what is before me.
ACCEPTANCE IS MY STRENGTH.

"When life hands you shit, fertilize a garden."
- *The Sense About Madness* by
Alyssa K. Vine-Hodge

Day 23

Truth:

EFFORTLESS EXISTENCE

What I take into consideration and focus on will increase. What I want to do and how I want my life to be remembered is what excites me. My existence is intentional and not based on survival. Albert Einstein thrived because he took action, he discovered theories on relativity and photoelectric effect that made history. He existed and put work in, until it became effortless. When I do this consistently, not only does the work become effortless, the blessings start to flow as well. Blessings are authorized to flow in my life as much as the oceans waves crash onto the shore....effortlessly. My breath continuously moves, effortlessly, I need not to remind my body to do this. I will recognize my special talents, and my effort will become effortless through my daily practice. My thoughts become my reality. For this to be an effortless victory in my history, I wake my intellect up from its slumber and make conscious habits. Today I will be like Albert Einstein and take action, the result will be an effortless, elated mental evolution.

"What we think, we become."
- Buddha

Day 24

Truth:

I AM GROUNDED

The earth is more than a garden. God made the
earth as my charging ground….
to feed me, to nourish me, and even heal me. Being barefoot
and one with the soil reduces inflammation and gives me
energy. This connection resembles a cellular phone plugged
into an outlet to recharge. Mother Earth is a power source
that reminds me that I am linked, as if I am a tree rooted
deep within the layers of clay. In order for me to be
spiritually grounded and capable of standing strong, it is
imperative that I remember to stay rooted. Tree branches
and leaves may sway when the wind or storms come, yet the
tree remains sound. Some may bend over time due to the
forces of nature, but they endure and stay solid since they
are grounded. Today, I will be one with earth, tapping into
its buried treasures that reveal the invigorating elements in
order for me to go deeper. My bare, naked feet will touch
the surface of this domain to recharge my body and ground
my soul. No matter what air, fire, or water may assemble,
I am joined with the element earth.
I AM GROUNDED.

Truth:

FEAR IS A CHOICE

FEAR: F is for False, E is for Evidence,
A is for Appearing, and R is for Real.
Fear is false evidence appearing real and a choice I can
make to live in or not. I have nothing to prove (verify,
justify, validate) to anyone but myself. I can focus on all the
remarkable possibilities that are before me and not allow
fear to keep me from becoming the highest quality version
of myself. Fear cannot touch me, yet it can rob me of so
much joy in my life if I give into it. Instead of consenting to
fear, I will use my power by choosing to be courageous and
reach for my best life. Today I will not let fear have a grip
on me. I will push past anxiety, and make the decision to be
brave and unafraid.

Ralph Waldo Emerson said it best:
"Nothing can bring you peace but yourself."

Truth:

POWER PLACEMENT

Power is the fuel we feed upon, or the source that supplies the drive and energy to accomplish work. A power source is necessary for electricity and to turn a car on.

Power is also given to where I choose to place it. If I misplace my energy by directing power to others, such as letting their words rule over me, I'll be like a car that has run out of gas on the side of the road waiting for someone else to supply more. I do not need for someone else to bring me fuel if I go to the main source, like a gas station, and fill up as often as needed. If I learn where the real power is? Then I won't be confused and run out of gas. Where do I place power? Who or what do I give power to?

The influence I allow in my life….

whether it be friends, church, work, politics, school, the internet, celebrities, and so on affects where

I place my power source.

Today, my intention is to know my

power source and feed it wisely.

Truth:

I AM HEALTHY

Some say that health is wealth, and indeed I agree with this. Just like plants that need sun and water to thrive, my health needs to be tended to and nourished daily. Health even contains the word 'heal.' If a leaf falls off a plant, it heals by growing another one. If my health is jeopardized, I need rest to help the healing process for whichever aspect of my health is afflicted. To be healthy, I must be willing to heal.
The five pillars of health are mental, spiritual, physical, financial, and social. These are the roots for the mind, spirit, body, money, and friends. Choosing to be healthy is taking the time to read or learn, time to pray, time to be physically active, time to work in ordered to get paid, and time to get to know people in order to develop a relationship.
Where do I want to invest in my health the most today?
I am willing to grow stronger by supporting, maintaining, and finding balance for each pillar of my health.

Pillars of Health:	What they affect:	How to flourish them:
Mental	Mind	Read, learn something new
Spiritual	Spirit	Pray, meditate, serve others
Physical	Body	Be active, exercise, eat consciously
Financial	Money	Work, invest, sacrifice, and save
Social	Friends	Take time to get to know people, go out, have fun!

Day 28

Truth:

ABUNDANCE

Acknowledging my successes allows me to build upon them. I appreciate how far I have come, and I remain grateful for all the abundance I have encountered. Fortune always follows me, and I know this because I have plenty. Abundance surrounds me in my rest, my food, and my shelter. Today, my abundance will meet every circumstance with unlimited thoughts.
The below information contains amazing insight into the Sanskrit mantra on abundance:
"Om Shreem Mahalakshmiyei Namaha"
aka
"Om greetings to the great Goddess Lakshmi Fortune."
Also known as the Money Mantra, this soothing mantra has been recited to help one know and fortify their goals. It is named after the Goddess Lakshmias in Hindu mythology, who is the Goddess of Wealth, Prosperity, and *Abundance.*
It can be used as a prayer not only to gain financial prosperity, but also to give the intelligence and wisdom to enlighten the mind with understanding. Lakshmi is the personification of all that brings good fortune, prosperity, and beauty.

*Sanskrit is an ancient Indo-European language of India, in which the Hindu scriptures and classical Indian epic poems are written and from which many northern Indian languages are derived.

Day 29

Truth:

I AM YOU, YOU ARE ME

We are each other's reflection, like a looking glass that I gaze into casting back my own image. This is the manner of each person I meet….a return of the reflection of myself. What I think of others is how I view myself. What I choose to see and say about others is how I judge myself. This is why I always do my best to seek love and pursue to find the joy within others. It may not be the easiest route, yet it is the road I desire to walk. Maybe the mirror I reflect in others will challenge me to love myself (as much as I need to love myself) when I see my reflection in them.

Every individual's thought process is unique and has a different reality TV show going on in his/her mind. Today, I will observe why I notice flaws, weaknesses, struggles, racism, or irritating things in others. The core of this resides in the fact that I battle with what I am perceiving.

What do I notice in others first? Unfortunately or luckily, I am seeing my own reflection. Others represent the mirror I need to see in order to grow.

Day 30

Truth:

I LOVE ME

I crave to be loved. Honestly, who doesn't? Deep down within (past the imaginary walls I've learned to falsely accept) is the hunger to be loved. I will be aware of these delusive barriers, whether they camouflage themselves as: success; romantic relationships; or feeling attractive, enlightened, wealthy, brilliant, and creative. The truth is: I can love myself. I've known this since my arrival here on this temporary surface. I am love. I was created in love, and today I elect to rediscover this. I take comfort in how I can wrap myself in the warmth of acceptance, how it feels incredible to snuggle in worthiness. I will take myself out, perhaps to get coffee, eat, go to the movies, shop, or visit the library. Whatever it is I decide to do will be fun because I will be in good company….me. As I look in the mirror to admire how perfect I've been made and how attractive I am, I will say "I LOVE ME!" If this confrontation is challenging, I will repeat it every day until it rolls off my tongue with ease. Until I know the value of me and it reflects in all that I do.

Self-rejection is the biggest sin that I commit. Self-love is crucial, embracing how precious I am. I am learning through this life how to take comfort sitting in the stillness, or perchance organically dancing to the beat of my soul. My footsteps leave a holy imprint on this earth, even if the wind blows sand over the tangible steps or the ocean waves wash them away, the authentic evidence is that I am here. The breath I breathe is here for this season and will eventually pass, so let me not tread lightly upon this path. Nobody will ever abuse me more than I have abused myself. The limit of my self-abuse is exactly the limit that I will tolerate from someone else. I am valuable and an irreplaceable asset to the universe.

Today, I choose to love, which allows my mind to be one with God. If I turn away from love, pain sets in. To think with love is to live, and to live starts with loving me.

"To love at all is to be vulnerable. Love anything, and your heart will certainly be wrung and possibly be broken."
- *The Four Loves* by C.S. Lewis

Smile!

It looks good on you.

57051453R00042

Made in the USA
Middletown, DE
27 July 2019